Unsupervised Thoughts

Where is my mind today?

R.L. Studios

2018

©

1

These Thoughts

Belong to _______________________________

Journaling has a charming effect

Healing may use reflection and mindfulness observations by seeking words to describe our goals, strengths, weakness, thoughts, feelings, actions, and attitudes. We may write about our pains, ambitions and dreams, aggressively, patiently or sensitively. Paper takes all types of ink, and any colours. We may express our ability to perceive and process our inner selves by constructing awareness of life experiences.

We may conclude ideas and re-build self-esteem, self-confidence, and self-determination by reactivating memories, thoughts and moments.
We can clarify by journaling. We can heal, learn, organize, transform, change, create, meditate, recall, imagine, improve, build, re-build, and restore our lives by journaling.

Self-Care

We sometimes care about others and easily forget about ourselves.
Self-care is care provided by you to yourself. You must love and care about yourself first before you care about anybody else.
You must identify beneficial needs and wants, and fulfill your desires and wishes. You must assure yourself that you are healthy physically, mentally, emotionally, and spiritually.

You must connect with nature, write a card to a love one, get a massage, meditate in your favorite place, exercise regularly, breath fresh and clean air, listen to music, enjoy a great book, watch a good movie, have fun, spoil yourself with things you can afford, energize yourself with a balanced diet, sleep well, take a nap and rest your body and mind, learn something new, and laugh with true friends.

Date: ______________________________

My Journal

Date: ____

Making Decisions

Any decision we make is ultimately our decision.

Every day we make wise, average, or poor decisions. Every morning we decide to move on with our daily routine or do something different.

Sometimes we decide things without much thinking, and sometimes we pause and think about what will be the best decision. We may move automatically like every other day, or we may reflect about the decision to make.

Decision making may be facilitated by emotional, physical, or spiritual experiences, by measuring options and consequences, by perception of pros and cons, by acquiring brainstorming knowledge, by revising and reviewing, by describing and planning, and by values, needs, attitudes, and behaviors.

Did you decide to pursue your personal goals, desires and dreams with a clear-headed mind?

____

____

____

____

____

____

____

____

My Journal

Date: _______________________________

Mindfulness is now

Mindfulness is the state of being conscious, completely awake, and fully attentive to the internal and external elements of the present moment.

When we are awake from our daily automatic life, we start living what appears to be a surreal dimension of reality. We understand and appreciate the interconnection of everything without judging or falling for life distractions (e.g. politics, sports, organized religion).

We have insight and we are insight of the present moment. When we achieve a sublime mindfulness approach to life, we experience great freedom and quality of living. We are no longer conditioned to act and react on auto-pilot.

We make wiser choices because we are _awake_. The practice of mindfulness assists us to identify and increase self- control and awareness of impulsive, automatically destructive, addictive, risky behaviors.

Do you have awareness of your thoughts, attitudes and behaviours?

My Journal

Date: ____

Balanced life

A balanced life is a life well lived.

We seek balance in so many aspects of our lives because we want to feel free of stress, and enjoy the elements of this world with a clear mind set. We must look at our life and fully understand its blue print, purpose and direction.

We must assess our goals, plans, and objectives and reflect about how to accomplish them by balancing external (e.g. work, family, friendships, responsibilities) and internal (e.g. health, mind, gratification, self-reward) forces.

Our true happiness is always shaped by balance.

We must empower and motivate ourselves in order to be free of conflicts. Let go of worries and keep feeding joy and harmony into your life.

Is your life balanced?

____

____

____

____

____

____

____

____

My Journal

Date: ___________________________________

Relationships

Relationships are necessary in our society.

Healthy relationships have a great impact in the prevention of conflict. We may or may not have a healthy relationship with ourselves, our family, our co-workers, or with our partner.

Our perceptions about our healthy or unhealthy relationships may vary with our belief system and the level of acceptance or denial. Unhealthy relationships sometimes deliver enough force of shame, guilt, frustration, pain, resentment, and annoyance to give up harmony and hope.

A healthy connection between people must be based on mutual respect, trust, loyalty, good communication, honesty, and a sense of own identity and care.

What makes a healthy relationship?

____

____

____

____

____

____

____

____

Date: ___________________________________

My Journal

Date: ______________________________

____

____

____

____

____

____

____

____

____

____

____

____

____

____

____

____

____

____

____

My Journal

Date: _______________________________

My Journal

Date: ____

My Journal

Date: _______________________________

Lifestyle

A lifestyle is a way of living and a way of life with certain habits, attitudes, morals, principles, economic status, and other aspects that may shape an individual or a group.

Sometimes people need to change everything in order to remain free of trouble. The changes may include employment, friendships, location, environment, diet, belief system, partnerships, relationships, and other aspects that have directly or indirectly impact on their lives.

Are you happy with your lifestyle?

My Journal

Date: ____

My Journal

Date: ___________________________________

My Journal

Date: ___________________________________

My Journal

Date: _______________________________

Assertiveness

Assertive people are able to communicate their thoughts, needs, and feelings without offending others.

Assertive people respect others rights and their own rights, and do not deny the right of others.

Passive people tend to the needs of others before their own needs.

Aggressive people definitely believe in their own rights but do not believe others have rights too.

*I am*____

____

____

____

____

____

____

____

____

____

____

My Journal

Date: ______________________________

My Journal

Date: _______________________________________

My Journal

Date: ____________________________

Date: _______________________________________

____

____

____

____

____

____

____

____

____

____

____

____

____

____

____

____

Unsupervised Thoughts

Feelings

When we feel, we liberate life to its most beautiful human form. Feelings connect us to each other and to the universe. We are able to feel when we allow ourselves to receive the full magic and energy from life. Feelings are not good or bad, they are the amplitude of our needs.

We can deeply engage in the process of self-discovery when we clarify our awareness and understanding about why we feel a certain way.

How do you feel today?

Awe	Aggravated	Caring	Blessed	Relieved
Delighted	Disgruntled	Stimulated	Courageous	Inspired
Playful	Adventurous	Yearning	Disturbed	Tender
Calm	Contempt	Empathy	Grateful	Angry
	Cynical	Fascinated	Guilt	Miserable
Thrusting	Valiant	Useless	Helpless	Overwhelmed
Excited	Furious	Discouraged	Hesitant	Perplexed
Accepting	Afraid	Appreciative	Humbled	Dread
Enthusiastic	Frustrated	Disappointed	Impotent	Puzzled
Engaged	Irritated	Anxious	Incapable	Detached
Eager	Disturbed	Anguish	Joy	Helpful
Relaxed	Daring	Indifferent	Nervous	Passive
Renewed	Determined	Isolated	Panic	Aggressive
Free	Grouchy	Grief	Perplexed	Troubled
Ecstatic	Edgy	Depressed	Powerless	Curious
Fulfilled	Hostile	Heartbroken	Questioning	Withdrawn
Happy	Impatient	Hopeless	Rejecting	Uncomfortable
Invigorated	Irate	Lonely	Reluctant	Embarrassed
Rejuvenated	Confident	Distant	Remorseful	Intense
Content	Disdain	Intrigued	Sad	Jealous
Vibrant	Warm	Lucky	Safe	Detached
Satisfied	Proud	Resistant	Scared	Insecure
Radiant	Brave	Aloof	Self-loving	Open
Amazed	Agitated	Affectionate	Sensitive	Peaceful
Lively	Moody	Longing	Shocked	Zestful
Mindful	Outraged	Melancholy		Mischievous
Refreshed	Capable	Bored	Sorry	Alert
Motivated	Resentful	Sorrow	Suspicious	Goofy
Serene	Strong	Uneasy	Terrified	Distant
Bliss	Bitter	Compassion	Thankful	Tranquil
Patient	Upset	Unhappy	Ungrounded	Amorous
Peaceful	Vindictive	Weary	Unsure	Friendly
Thrilled	Worthy	Ashamed	Worried	Distracted
Concerned	Annoyed	Surprised	Proud	Loved

My Journal

Date: ___________________________________

My Journal

Date: ___________________________________

My Journal

Date: ___________________________________

____

____

____

____

____

____

____

____

____

____

____

____

____

____

____

____

Resolving Problems

We will encounter problems during our lives. Sometimes we will have minor problems, and sometimes unthinkable problems.

Problems exist, and we are able to resolve them by first identifying symptoms of the problem, seeking information about the problem, brainstorming answers for the problem, choosing the most beneficial resolution for the problem, visualizing and clarifying a plan to resolve the problem, reviewing the proposal to resolve the problem, and putting in action the most positive solution for the problem.

I resolve problems by _______________________________

____

____

____

____

____

____

____

____

____

My Journal

Date: _______________________________

My Journal

Date: _______________________________

My Journal

Date: ___________________________

My Journal

Date: ___________________________________

My Journal

Date: _______________________________

Spiritual Journey

How we view our own existence in the universe is what makes us aware of our actions and reactions to everything.

Our physical existence constantly reinvents its time and connects our bodies and souls to the universe. We are the energy that the universe uses to magically and patiently evolve through us. Our bodies are a process that never stands still, and our souls are vessels seeking enlightenment by connecting and feeling the world physically, socially, emotionally, and spiritually.

Our souls constantly animate our bodies and seek balance, harmony, meaning, serenity, purpose, self-actualization, and satisfaction.

We are the mindfulness conscience that brings change by letting go of our old limited beliefs. We meditate and seek positive change in our inner selves by embracing our body and soul towards the awakening of compassion, empathy, goodness, and love.

We are souls using bodies. We belong to the multi-level dimensions of the universe.

____

____

____

____

____

____

____

My Journal

Date: ______________________________________

My Journal

Date: _______________________________

My Journal

Date: ______________________________________

What we are

We are what we think, and our thoughts can be believable to us and others. We have a blue print to follow and determine where our life must go.

We must see our lives not as an idea of living, but as a reality to accomplish. Our dreams, plans, and goals have more reasons for us to pursue them, than to let them fade away.

We must embrace basic principles and deeply believe in ourselves.

My Journal

Date: ______________________________

My Journal

Date: ___________________________________

My Journal

Date: ____

My Journal

Date: ______________________________

My Journal

Date: _______________________________

My Journal

Date: _______________________________

Change

Change is not always wanted, accepted, or respected.

We must connect with our emotions in order to understand our actions, and modify our behaviours. We must not ignore our needs to avoid changing our destructive behaviours.

We must not forget the execution of forgiveness to avoid change. Change is what connects the universe, and we are part of it.

Accept, embrace, and understand that change is a beneficial element of life.

My Journal

Date: _______________________________

My Journal

Date: _______________________________

My Journal

Date: ______________________________

My Journal

Date: ________________________________

We must be assertive in order to increase control of our lives. We must be clear about what we want, fair, consistent, honest, confident, flexible and able to compromise.

You may want to apply these simple rules:

- Do not apologize or explain if you don't have to
- Use eye contact and calm voice
- Wait for your turn to speak
- Be clear, honest, and direct
- Recognize others rights and compromise if necessary or possible
- Don't except to convince
- Accept that life is not fair
- Be flexible and accept consequences
- Do not make excuses
- Pause and decide before replying
- Be aware of your body posture
- Be mindfulness of your surroundings
- Use I statements when necessary
- Do not be afraid to say No
- Be humble and firm
- Apply positive attitude
- Be knowledgeable about the subject of conversation
- Think before you open your mouth
- Select timing for conversations and environment
- Pay attention to details
- Value relationships and understand others stressors
- Validate others perceptions, valuable observations, and comments
- Agree and disagree without yelling or with an aggressive posture
- Ask for clarification when necessary
- Listen and focus what is actually being said
- Remain focus on the subject of discussion
- Acknowledge when you are wrong and apologize
- Select the level of your assertiveness with situation and person
- Positively practice what you had learned

- **Always show respect and self-control**
- **Be polite and cooperate**
- **Understand others perceptions and attributes**
-
-
-
-
-
-
-
-
-
-
-
-
-
-

Remember your life is your life

My Journal

Date: ___________________________________

My Journal

Date: _______________________________

My Journal

Date: ___________________________

My Journal

Date: _______________________________

____

____

____

____

____

____

____

____

____

____

____

____

____

____

____

____

____

My Journal

Date: _______________________________

My Journal

Date: ______________________________

My Journal

Date: ___________________________________

My Journal

Date: ______________________________

My Journal

Date: _______________________________

My Journal

Date: ______________________________

My Journal

Date: ______________________________

My Journal

Date: _______________________________

Life

Life sometimes brings us unthinkable pain due to grief and loss. We may lose a loved one, a close relationship, a pet, a friend, a job, a lover, our own health, or something or someone we care a lot for. We may feel angry, depressed, anxious, and dreamlike.

We may avoid feelings of sadness and despair by taking the path of denial, which may result in substance abuse, mental illness, and health problems. We neglect ourselves and others, and question our ways mentally and spiritually. We may feel lost in the realm wheel of magic, test the boundaries of sanity, and our capacity to remain human.

Loss may change our ways of thinking, and generate emotions and physical reactions that we had never experienced.

Grief is a natural reaction to loss. Grief can take away our sense of belonging to something or someone, and we may feel sad, scared, and lonely. People grieve differently, depending on their life experiences, personality traits, faith, learned coping skills, support system, type of loss, or other factors.

My Journal

Date: ___________________________

My Journal

Date: ______________________________

My Journal

Date: ___________________________________

My Journal

Date: _______________________________

My Journal

Date: _______________________________

My Journal

Date: _______________________________

My Journal

Date: ________________________________

My Journal

Date: ______________________________________

My Journal

Date: _______________________________________

My Journal

Date: _________________________________

My Journal

Date: ___________________________________

My Journal

Date: _______________________________

My Journal

Date: _______________________________

My Journal

Date: ___________________________________

My Journal

Date: ___________________________

My Journal

Date: ___________________________________

My Journal

Date: ___________________________

Date: _______________________________

My Journal

Date: ___________________________________

My Journal

Date: ____

Be Like Water

Water does not fight its way but finds a way.

If you drop an open bottle of water on the floor, the water will not break the floor. The water will go around and into everything until it finds its destiny in a soft and calm way.

Adjusting to everything is a sublime experience. Accepting first that life is unfair is true awareness. Deciding to become part of your blue print or destiny is genuine understanding of your life purpose.

Increasing self-responsibility and self-accountability helps master and acquire self-determination. You are the shape of your thoughts and your actions are the results of such process.

No more blaming, no more excuses, no more denial, no more justification, rationalizations, or minimizations. No more lies.

Apply what you know to be beneficial to you, and to what you love and care.

My Journal

Date: _______________________________

My Journal

Date: ___________________________________

My Journal

Date: _______________________________

My Journal

Date: _______________________________

My Journal

Date: _______________________________

My Journal

Date: _______________________________

My Journal

Date: _______________________________

My Journal

Date: ___________________________

My Journal

Date: _______________________________________

My Journal

Date: ______________________________

My Journal

Date: ______________________________

My Journal

Date: ___________________________

My Journal

Date: ___________________________________

My Journal

Date: ___________________________________

My Journal

Date: ______________________________

My Journal

Date: ___________________________________

My Journal

Date: ___________________________

My Journal

Date: _______________________________

My Journal

Date: ___________________________________

My Journal

Date: ___________________________________

My Journal

Date: ___________________________________

My Journal

Date: ________________________________

My Journal

Date: ___________________________________

My Journal

Date: _______________________________

I care about

Think about what and who you deeply care

I care about____.

I care about____.

I care about____.

I care about____.

I care about____.

I care about____.

I care about____.

I care about____.

I care about____.

I care about____.

I care about____.

I care about____.

I care about____.

I care about____.

I care about____.

I care about____.

I care about____.

I care about____.

I care about____.

My Journal

Date: ___________________________

My Journal

Date: ______________________________

My Journal

Date: ________________________________

My Journal

Date: ______________________________

I need

Think about what you really need.

I need ____.

I need ____.

I need ____.

I need ____.

I need ____.

I need ____.

I need ____.

I need ____.

I need ____.

I need ____.

I need ____.

I need ____.

I need ____.

I need ____.

I need ____.

I need ____.

I need ____.

I need ____.

I need ____.

And Then?

www.ingramcontent.com/pod-product-compliance
Lightning Source LLC
Chambersburg PA
CBHW081837250726
48659CB00008B/2486